LUNCH AT THE ZOO

JOYCE ALTMAN

LUNCH AT THE ZOO

WHAT ZOO ANIMALS EAT AND WHY

Foreword by
Dr. Ellen Dierenfeld

Illustrations by
RICK CHRUSTOWSKI

HENRY HOLT AND COMPANY · NEW YORK

With special thanks to the following people for all of their invaluable help and encouragement: Dr. Ellen Dierenfeld, head, Department of Wildlife Nutrition, Bronx Zoo/Wildlife Conservation Society; Dr. Dan Wharton, director, Central Park Wildlife Center; Frank Indiviglio, supervisor, Animal Department, Prospect Park Wildlife Center; Barbara Toddes, nutrition program manager, Philadelphia Zoo; Jay Kilgore, lead animal keeper, Los Angeles Zoo; Pam Manning, senior veterinary technician, Bronx Zoo; Dennis DeMello, staff photographer, Bronx Zoo; Diane Shapiro, media services archivist, Bronx Zoo; Bill Meng, retired staff photographer, Bronx Zoo; Mary Forde, photo librarian, Philadelphia Zoo; Linda Countryman, docent, Los Angeles Zoo; Harvey Fischer; Theresa Prator; Sue Spencer; and Sue Maher. I would also like to thank my editors, Reka Simonsen, Margaret Garrou, and Laura Godwin; my agent at Sterling Lord Literistic, George Nicholson; and Debbie Harris, Judith Whipple, Barbara Bader, and Amos the Amazon parrot (who sang cheerfully in the Highland Falls, New York, library while I transcribed).

Henry Holt and Company, LLC, *Publishers since 1866*
115 West 18th Street, New York, New York 10011

Henry Holt is a registered trademark of Henry Holt and Company, LLC
Text copyright © 2001 by Joyce Altman
Illustrations copyright © 2001 by Rick Chrustowski
All rights reserved.
Published in Canada by Fitzhenry & Whiteside Ltd.,
195 Allstate Parkway, Markham, Ontario L3R 4T8.

Library of Congress Cataloging-in-Publication Data
Altman, Joyce.
Lunch at the zoo: what zoo animals eat and why / Joyce Altman; illustrations by Rick Chrustowski
p.   cm.
Summary: Describes how zoo nutritionists learn what to feed the animals in their care,
the feeding procedures used by large zoos, and the nutritional needs of a variety of zoo animals.
1. Zoo animals—Feeding and feeds—Juvenile literature.   [1. Zoo animals—Feeding and feeds.
2. Animals—Food habits.]   I. Chrustowski, Rick, ill.   II. Title.
QL77.5.A435   2000   636.088'9—dc21   00-22430

ISBN 0-8050-6070-7   First Edition—2001   Designed by Nicole Stanco
Printed in Mexico
The artist used pencil on watercolor paper to create the illustrations for this book.
1   3   5   7   9   10   8   6   4   2

Permission to use the following photographs is gratefully acknowledged: page 14, copyright © Philadelphia Zoo / Bill Buchanan; page iii (top), copyright © Wildlife Conservation Society headquartered at the Bronx Zoo / Dennis DeMello; pages iii (bottom), 16, 25, 32, 35, 51, 55, 59, 61, 63, 67, 70, copyright © Wildlife Conservation Society headquartered at the Bronx Zoo; pages 20, 29, copyright © Wildlife Conservation Society headquartered at the Bronx Zoo / Bill Meng.

APR - - 2001

For my husband, Billy;
my daughter, Emma;
and my mother, Marion

CONTENTS

LUNCH AT THE ZOO

FOREWORD

Zoo nutrition is a field of science involving the proper feeding of zoo animals. While many nutritionists focus on just one type of animal, or species, zoo nutritionists are responsible for creating healthful diets for hundreds of different animals. To do our jobs properly, we must be knowledgeable about the anatomies, behaviors, and body chemistries of many kinds of mammals, reptiles, and birds.

Using successful diets developed by experienced animal caretakers as starting points, the zoo nutritionist's job is to improve and understand the science of animal nutrition. Those of us in the field often work together to communicate what we learn. Sharing what we know about diets, products, and feeding techniques is a key part of advancing the field of zoo-animal nutrition.

To feed zoo animals, we must also be open to the lessons of nature. In zoos, we can rarely feed animals what they would eat in the wild. We *can,* however, offer substitute diets containing the same basic nutrients. We constantly bear in mind that a diet must not only be good for an animal but also has to be appealing. Feeding behaviors may not simply be dictated by nutrition. Taste, texture, smell, size, shape, color, and even movement are all important facets of our feeding programs, at times even more important than the actual makeup of an animal's diet.

Making the science of nutrition a part of the overall care of wild animals within a zoo gives us exciting and ongoing challenges. This book provides a helpful insight into many of the issues we face as we continue to try to understand the role that nutrition plays in animal health, reproduction, and ultimately, wildlife conservation.

Dr. Ellen Dierenfeld, Ph.D., CNS
Head, Department of Wildlife Nutrition
Bronx Zoo/Wildlife Conservation Society

INTRODUCTION

In the wild, animals learn how to take care of themselves and can usually find the foods that are right to eat. Sometimes they are taught by their parents what is good for them and what is not. In nature, a parrot knows which leaves, fruits, or seeds are good and how to find and open them; a lion learns how to hunt down, capture, and eat a gazelle; a fishing eagle knows how to swoop into the water and grab a fish with its talons (claws). As long as an animal's habitat (the place where it lives) is not disturbed by natural or other causes, the animal is usually able to find food and survive.

Sadly, however, many animals' habitats have been disturbed, and more and more creatures are losing their homes in the wild. Zoos are increasingly becoming places that protect and save wild animals. As a result, how zoo animals are fed and cared for is becoming extremely important to their survival.

But how do animals that live in zoos manage to get the right foods? They can't go out and search for their own meals, and some aren't raised by their parents, so they haven't always been taught what to eat. Instead they have to depend on the people who care for them to provide the proper food. Animal managers study what the animals need to keep them healthy and well nourished, because they know that good nutrition is very important to good health.

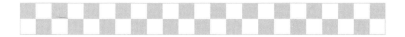

CHAPTER ONE

WHAT DO YOU FEED AN ARCTIC FOX?

You'd think that feeding zoo animals would be simple—they would just be given the same things they eat in the wild. But that's not how it works, for a number of reasons. For one thing, the zoo may not know exactly what the animals' wild diets would be. Or the natural foods they eat may not be available to buy or can't be grown nearby. For instance, in a cold climate you can't grow the same grasses that grow in Africa.

Nutrients and Their Roles

Nutrient	Function	Sources
Protein	Forms skin, fur, nails, muscles, and most other body tissues; repairs the body and helps it grow	Meat, insects, fish, eggs, milk, seeds, grains, beans
Carbohydrates	Combine with oxygen to release energy for the body to do its work	Hay, leaves, vegetables, fruits, grains, nectars
Fat	Stores energy from food; supplies energy to muscles; helps keep the skin healthy and the body warm	Meat, oil, nuts, seeds, egg yolk

Vitamins	Help release energy from proteins, carbohydrates, and fats; help the body protect itself against disease	Various plant and animal sources; commercial supplements
Minerals	Help build bones, teeth, and blood; regulate blood clotting and the heartbeat; maintain proper balance of body fluids; help the blood carry oxygen to the cells	Various plant and animal sources; commercial supplements
Water	Controls body temperature; helps with blood circulation; carries nutrients to the cells; gets rid of wastes	

So how do zoos know exactly what—and how much—to feed their animals? And how do they find substitutes for the animals' natural diets?

The people who take care of animals at zoos—the curators, keepers, and veterinarians—work together to make sure that all diets meet the needs of the animals they are intended for. Zoos are very careful about what they feed their animals. All food is checked both for quality and for the nutrients it provides. Because of this, it's very important that zoo visitors don't try to feed the animals, as doing so can easily upset their diets and make them ill.

Some zoos even have a special person on staff, called a nutritionist, who reviews the zoo diets and makes sure that they are wholesome. A healthful diet provides all the nutrients an animal needs. Nutrients are the parts of food—the proteins, carbohydrates, fats, vitamins, minerals, and water—that keep animals healthy (see pages

10–11). Nutritionists find out what nutrients an animal needs, then create a diet using this information. They try to make sure that zoo diets are as healthful as wild diets.

What Does an Orangutan Eat?

Suppose a zoo is opening an exhibit for orangutans, which are large, red-haired apes from Southeast Asia. How do the caretakers know what to feed them?

Zoo nutritionists and curators do research to find out what's best to feed an animal. First they look at the zoo's records to see what kind of diet has been used in the past and if it has been successful. If the animal has never lived in the zoo before, they get in touch with other zoos that have had that species. Nutritionists also read whatever has been written about the animal's feeding habits in the wild.

Orangutans' large teeth and jaws help them to crack hard nuts, grind bark, and open spiny, thick-skinned fruits.

In many cases, what's known about the feeding of farm animals (such as chickens, cows, and sheep) and pets (such as dogs, cats, and rabbits) can be applied to zoo animals. The nutritional needs of lions and tigers, for example, aren't really that different from those of your own house cat, and the wolf's diet isn't too far removed from your pet dog's.

Sometimes the only way for scientists to know just what nutrients an animal really needs in its diet is to travel to the animal's homeland. Once there, the scientist will track the animal, observe the various foods it eats, and bring food samples back to the laboratory to be analyzed by nutritionists for exact nutrient content. Whenever possible, blood samples are also taken to learn even more about the animal. The end results can make a big difference to the health of captive animals. While research such as this is extremely helpful, it's also very expensive and time-consuming, and so it can be done only for zoo animals about which the least is known.

On some occasions, nutritionists themselves get

Giant pandas eat more then thirty pounds of bamboo leaves and stems
daily. They usually sit while eating.

the chance to go into the field to do such research. For example, Dr. Ellen Dierenfeld, who heads the Department of Wildlife Nutrition at the Bronx Zoo, has had the opportunity to study several endangered animals firsthand, including giant pandas in China, black rhinoceroses in Africa, and black-footed ferrets in Wyoming. Endangered animals are those that are in danger of dying out, or becoming extinct.

So how do zoos know what to feed an orangutan? As it turns out, scientists have had the opportunity to study and record this animal's eating habits in the wild. They know that the orangutan's wild diet consists of fruits, some bark and leaves, and birds' eggs. In captivity, a substitute diet would include special primate biscuits (similar to breakfast cereal and containing all the nutrients the animal needs), fruits, vegetables, and browse (leaves, shoots, twigs, and other vegetation often gathered from around the zoo).

Are Zoo Animals Fussy Eaters?

Some zoo animals are good eaters, but others can be very picky. It's really the same for animals as it is for you. If someone offers you food that looks unfamiliar or not very tasty, you probably won't want to try it, even if you're told how good it is. Similarly, it doesn't do any good to offer a healthful meal to an animal if it doesn't taste or look good to it. The animal simply won't eat the food if it doesn't find it appealing.

Food presentation—the shape apple pieces are cut into, the size of a fish that's being offered, how feeding dishes are placed in an exhibit (on the floor or ten feet up in a tree)—is very important. Different things trigger animals to eat, such as texture, color, smell, whether the food is warm or cold, and if it's alive or not. It can take days or weeks before an animal will start eating a new type of food, and it may never eat it at all. A variety of different foods is usually offered at once so that there is always something that will appeal. When careful attention is paid to the animals' needs, the right foods and presentation can be found.

Zoo Kitchens

Since zoos feed thousands of animals every day, buying, storing, and preparing food is a very big job. Some large zoos have a special purchasing department in which the staff is responsible for ordering food for all the animals. At smaller zoos this job is usually left up to the nutritionist.

When the food arrives, most of it is stored in either a food commissary (which is a giant kitchen) or a warehouse connected to food-storage rooms, depending on the zoo. In the storage rooms are all kinds of foods. There may be huge bins filled with

Hundreds of meals are prepared each day by zookeepers, who follow exact directions to make sure that the nutritional needs of all the animals are met.

dry foods such as mixed-grain pellets and biscuits, bird pellets, and high-protein kibble; shelves of canned feline (cat), canine (dog), and primate (monkey and ape) foods; packages of cereal (including baby cereal); peanut butter; rice; nuts and seeds; and vitamins and other supplements. Some zoos even have special barns where various kinds of hay are stored. In the commissary, there are also walk-in refrigerators and freezers that hold the large amounts of meat, fish, chicken, and produce (fruits and vegetables) that are delivered several times a week.

Food is washed in large stainless-steel sinks and prepared on gigantic counters. A zoo kitchen has other equipment as well, such as scales for weighing food, restaurant-sized kettles and rice cookers, salad shredders and food grinders, and various knives and chopping blocks. The staff keeps everything spotlessly clean and sterilizes cooking pans and utensils by washing them in dishwashers.

Where Zoo Food Comes From

Much of the meat, poultry, fish, and produce that zoos purchase comes from the same vendors that restaurants and hotels use. Zoo animals are fed the same high-quality food that people eat. The only difference is that zoos may use slightly misshapen food that restaurants might pass up. Some things, such as horse meat or certain types of fish that people don't eat, are bought from exotic-animal suppliers. Special suppliers also sell canned foods, dried pellets, animal biscuits, and such small animals as mice, rats, crickets, mealworms, earthworms, and minnows. Three to six different sizes of rats and mice are purchased to meet the needs of different animals, from tiny "pinkies" to slightly larger "fuzzies" to full-grown mice and rats. Zoos also need to buy large amounts of hay, and they generally buy several varieties from nearby farms.

When foods arrive at the zoo, control checks are

made to be sure the quality is good and to confirm the nutritional content of some items. To check the nutritional content of hay, for instance, samples are taken to laboratories to be analyzed.

The rules that zoos follow for handling food are called protocols—many of which are similar to what you and your family do in your own home. These protocols include making sure that the food is handled carefully, so it stays clean, and storing it at the right temperature (refrigerating it if needed), so it stays fresh. It is also important that food handlers always wash their hands before working with food and when switching from one type of food to another. There are protocols for how long it's safe to store frozen fish and the proper way to thaw it, and also for how long cans of food can be kept in storage without spoiling.

At zoos, there is usually one main commissary from which all food is sent out. In some zoos, food is delivered to the various buildings from the commissary completely prepared so that keepers need only place the pans into each exhibit and remove them later that day or the next morning. The pans are then washed and sterilized. Other zoos have their commissary workers measure and weigh out all the food needed for the animals in each building, but the keepers do all cutting and preparing in their own special kitchens.

Diet Notebooks

At most zoos, such as the Bronx Zoo in New York City, there are chalkboards up in the kitchens that list the exact foods that need to be prepared for each of the animals. For example, an arctic fox's daily diet might read: 1 cup dry dog kibble, ¼ can feline diet (1 mouse replaces feline diet twice a week), special treat of ½ apple twice a week. The diet for this animal in the wild would be equally nutritious, but the ingredients would be different.

In the wild, arctic foxes live mostly on small mammals such as lemmings but may also eat birds, insects, and berries.

Depending on the season, an arctic fox might eat rodents such as lemmings and other small mammals, eggs, carrion (dead animals), and berries.

At the Philadelphia Zoo, instead of chalkboards, notebooks containing each animal's diet on separate sheets of paper are kept in all the buildings.

The sheets list the types and amounts of food to be included in the diet as well as vitamins and minerals, allowable food treats, and special needs, such as "treat logs" or bones to gnaw on. Within a species, though, some animals might be much bigger or smaller and so need different amounts of food. Also, animals sometimes have very strong likes and dislikes, and zoos try to keep these in mind. All of this is carefully written out in the notebooks. At zoos, large food mixtures are sometimes made a day in advance. The rest of the food is prepared very early in the morning—hours before the zoo opens to the public.

Food: Dead or Alive?

While many carnivorous (meat-eating) animals prefer to eat their food live, in zoos they are almost always taught to accept dead or prepared food. There's a good reason for this, which is that it's just not practical to have so much live food on hand. Keeping thousands of food animals alive takes up a lot of the keepers' time, since the animals have to be sheltered, fed, and humanely cared for. Also, it's very expensive. Another problem is that it's hard to keep track of live animals let loose in an exhibit, and they could actually harm the zoo animals by biting them.

Most zoo animals adjust to eating thawed-out frozen food or freshly killed food fairly easily. For snakes, however, the adjustment is sometimes difficult, and it can take a little time and effort on the keepers' part to get a snake to accept dead food. They may have to wiggle a mouse or a rat in front of a snake at each meal for a while to get it to eat. But since snakes tend to key in on scent more than on movement to find their food, it can be done. If a snake is new to captivity and is having trouble making the adjustment, it may be given live food for a short time.

For animals such as the giant anteater of

A giant anteater's tongue, which is wet but not sticky, extends as far as twenty-two inches to catch termites and other insects.

Central and South America, which in nature would eat as many as 35,000 ants and termites in a single day, a good substitute diet is necessary in captivity. It's simply not possible for zoos to keep this number of live insects on hand. Fortunately, captive anteaters will accept a gruel of cat or dog food soaked in water.

There are some animals, however, that never adjust to dead food. Most frogs and lizards, for instance, will not eat unless they see movement from their prey. To feed them, live earthworms and wax worms are bought in large quantities. The

worms are kept in special storage refrigerators in a
state of semi-hibernation so they don't need to be
fed themselves. Zoos also keep live insects on hand
for the lizards. In the wild, a lizard might feed on

With its excellent eyesight, a Parson's chameleon can shoot out its
sticky tongue to capture insects up to a body length away.

many different types of insects, each providing a little something different nutritionally. In the zoo, caretakers alternate the insects as much as possible to make sure the animals get all the nutrients they need, as well as to provide them with some variety, which keeps them active. In the summer, keepers often set traps and use nets to catch moths, caterpillars, and spiders, which are offered as special treats.

CHAPTER TWO

HOW DO YOU FEED A HUNGRY CROCODILE?

The number of meals zoo animals eat daily, or whether they eat every day at all, varies greatly from animal to animal. For instance, a tiny African dormouse, weighing only a few ounces, is fed a very small amount of food each day—a piece of kale leaf or other greens, one pellet of dry rodent chow, and a teaspoon of mixed seeds. That's all it needs. A ten-foot-long South American boa constrictor eats four to six rats every other week.

An Asian elephant uses its trunk for gathering food, drinking, smelling, and sometimes fighting. In zoos, elephants throw hay on their backs as protection from the sun and insects.

The zoo animal with the biggest appetite, the elephant, can consume up to two 100-pound bales of grass hay, ten pounds of mixed grains, some browse, a scoop of vitamin E powder, and special treats of carrots, apples, and loaves of bread—and that's just for one day.

Zoo animals are usually fed their main meal at night, for several good reasons. Keepers need to be able to safely move their animals, including the dangerous ones, such as lions, tigers, and bears, from their daytime exhibit areas to their night-time quarters. It's safer for the animals if they are inside at night, and it also gives the keepers the opportunity to clean the outdoor areas.

Since the animals are hungry at night and they know their food is waiting for them, it's easy for keepers to get them to come inside. Many zoo animals actually have two different living areas—the one you see when you visit the zoo, and one, usually behind it, that's hidden from public view.

While the animals are still outside, the keepers place their food in their nighttime off-exhibit quarters and then mechanically open a door that connects the two areas. Once the animals are safely inside and the door is closed, the keepers clean the daytime exhibit area so it will be ready for the animals the next morning. The nighttime off-exhibit area is cleaned when the animals are out for the day.

In addition to feeding and cleaning, there are two other reasons animals are taken off-exhibit at night. One is so keepers can observe them carefully. Off-exhibit areas are smaller, so keepers can get a good, close-up look at the animals to make sure they are healthy. The second reason is that many animals feel more secure in their own "bedroom" at night than they do in the open spaces of an exhibit.

The way feeding is done in zoos depends very much on the species involved. For instance, if a keeper needs to feed a mouse, he or she simply

Keepers can go right into California sea lion exhibits to feed the animals fish, which they swallow whole.

opens a small door at the back of the mouse's quarters and reaches in to place fresh pans of food and water inside and take out old pans.

Even for many larger animals, such as goats, de-scented skunks, and sea lions, going in to feed them generally isn't difficult because they aren't aggressive. But how do keepers manage to feed venomous snakes and hungry crocodiles, and how do they do it day after day without getting hurt?

Breakfast with the Snakes

Zookeepers have to take many precautions when they feed snakes, especially venomous snakes, which use poison to kill their prey. How, for instance, is a spitting cobra fed safely when its venom, aimed straight for the eyes, can cause blindness?

Venomous snakes are fed basically the same way as nonvenomous constrictor snakes, which kill their prey by wrapping their coils around it and suffocating it. But when keepers feed venomous snakes, extra safety measures are taken. For example, when feeding spitting cobras, keepers wear special goggles that cover their eyes completely. Even the venom of a baby spitting cobra is extremely dangerous.

In fact, before feeding any snake—venomous or constrictor—a reptile keeper will look through a window at the back of the snake's exhibit to make sure the animal isn't right at the door. If it's not, the keeper will open the door carefully and then place a mouse or rat inside. If it is, the keeper will come back later.

If several snakes live together, it's common for one to be left in the exhibit to eat while the others are removed to eat elsewhere. Keepers use special long snake hooks to move the snakes into separate barrels with tight-fitting lids. The snake's food will either be waiting for it in the barrel or is carefully put in with long tongs once the snake is already inside.

Since snakes usually eat only once a week or once every two weeks, this method, although it takes a lot of time, works best. Separating the snakes ensures that each one gets the right amount of food and a quiet place to eat. It also keeps them from harming each other while eating. Snakes'

Snakes that live in groups, such as this cobra, are carefully put into separate barrels to eat quietly on their own.

teeth point backward, and if two snakes were to latch onto the same mouse or rat to eat, it would be very hard for one of them to back off. Eventually the snake with the larger mouth would cover the mouth of the smaller snake. Most likely this would lead to fighting, puncture wounds, and possibly the larger snake eating the smaller one.

Some reptiles are very particular eaters. The Eastern hognose snake, for instance, eats only toads in the wild, and it doesn't usually like the other types of food fed to snakes. Since toads generally aren't available to be offered for food, keepers take dead mice and put them in a bag for a while with a live toad, which is called scenting the mice. Then the toad is taken out, unharmed. Some of the toad's scent gets on the mice, and the snake will then eat the mice, because they smell just like a toad. Although mice may not be the snake's favorite food, they seem to be acceptable, and they meet its nutritional needs as well as a toad would.

How Do You Feed a Two-Headed Snake?

Occasionally a very rare animal presents a challenge for zookeepers. At the Los Angeles Zoo, for example, there was once a two-headed gopher snake on exhibit, and when it was young, it required a special feeding method.

A barrier is placed between the two-headed snake's heads to keep them from grasping at the same food and harming each other.

Despite the fact that one of the snake's heads was more subordinate (passive) and the other more dominant (aggressive), keepers had to keep the two heads from grasping at the same food and hurting each other. They put a paper barrier between the two heads and only fed the dominant head its meal of mice once a week. The subordinate head, although it would sometimes try to reach the food, didn't need to eat since they shared the same stomach and the dominant head ate enough to fill the animal up. As the snake got older, it was fed once every two to three weeks, and eventually the two heads got used to this method and the barrier was no longer needed.

Lunch with the Crocodiles

It's not easy to move large crocodiles around, so they're usually fed together in their exhibit. Keepers can and do go in with the crocodiles, although they have to be very familiar with the individual animals because some can be more aggressive than others.

To avoid putting themselves in danger, keepers follow the same routine day after day, year after year. If they keep a safe distance from the animals and always feed and clean the exhibit the same way, the crocodiles will get used to them and will just stay in an area of the exhibit where they feel secure until the keepers leave. But to be safe, keepers always carry a long pole as they work, generally go into the exhibit two at a time, and never take their eyes off the animals.

Dinner with the Birds

Feeding animals that aren't dangerous is a lot simpler than feeding ones that are. Keepers can usually go right in and feed most birds without difficulty. To do so, they enter the birds' exhibits through small doors in the back. You probably haven't noticed these doors when you've visited zoos because they're painted on the inside to match the colors of the exhibit walls.

When many birds of the same species live together, zoos have to make sure that each bird gets its share of food. Sometimes they are all fed together and are given one type of food that's nutritionally complete. In other cases, the birds are given a variety of foods but are separated at feeding time and hand-fed some of the most nutritious items to make sure they each get enough. They are often separated if there are both dominant and subordinate birds within a group, in which case the dominant birds may gobble up more than their share of the most nutritious foods.

Sometimes a dominant bird in a large exhibit will follow a keeper around as food pans are put down, picking out its favorite foods. The favorites (such as grapes) often taste good but don't provide much nutrition. The passive birds, forced to eat the more nutritious but less tasty base diet that's left behind, may actually be healthier. One of the ways zoos have solved this problem is to cut the

This mixed-species exhibit consists of a Great Indian hornbill (top branch), two African finches (lower tree), a California quail (eating at ground level), and a crowned pigeon.

more desirable foods into tiny pieces and coat them with the base diet.

In many zoos, birds (and some other animals) live together in mixed-species exhibits. In the Bronx Zoo's JungleWorld building, for instance, several species of birds share living areas. Since they need to eat different foods, the keepers have to find ways to get each species to eat only what's meant for it. A common trick is to place feeding pans at varying heights and on varying perch sizes.

Some of the birds in JungleWorld also share their exhibits with large monitor lizards and pond turtles. So how do keepers make sure that each animal is getting the food it needs? First, they always place bird pans out of the reptiles' reach. Then, to avoid struggles between the monitor lizards and the pond turtles, they feed the turtles in the water and the monitors on land. To ensure that the turtles get enough to eat, their food (mice and fish) is cut into small enough pieces to swallow quickly so the lizards can't take it from them.

Hiding Special Treats

Zoos often use food to keep animals busy and alert. This kind of stimulation is very important to an animal's well-being. In the wild, most animals will spend a lot of their time and energy searching for food. Many zoos now hide food throughout exhibits so the animals can keep busy trying to find it. At the Philadelphia Zoo, nutritious primate biscuits and bits of peanut butter are scattered throughout the lowland-gorilla exhibits for the apes to find. This is in addition to their regular diet of vegetables, leaves, and fruits. The keepers also hide crickets and mealworms inside an earthen pit in the sloth bears' exhibit once a week. And several times a week they put dabs of peanut butter and honey on the trees for the bears to find.

At the Bronx Zoo, the gibbons have a special feeding tree filled with peanuts. When keepers activate the tree, a few nuts fall out. The gibbons

To keep lowland gorillas busy and active, peanut butter and primate biscuits are hidden throughout their exhibit.

come by often to check for the treats, and from time to time they find some. Also at the Bronx Zoo, grizzly bears have a special tree in their exhibit that is set on a timer to release honey every so often, which is a favorite snack.

Bears in the Woodland Park Zoo in Seattle, Washington, the San Diego Zoo in California, and the Central Park Zoo in New York City can go fishing for live trout. The Central Park Zoo's polar bears also search for berries that are hidden in a large snowbank created by ice machines that are hidden above their exhibit.

DO ANIMALS NEED VITAMINS?

No matter how nutritious the diets of zoo animals are, the animals often need to be given extra vitamins and minerals to make sure that they stay in peak health. Just as you may eat good, healthful foods and still your parents might tell you to take your multivitamin pill, animals sometimes have to take vitamin supplements, too.

Vitamins are actually natural substances found in plants and animals that help the body carry on all the processes needed to sustain life. If an animal eats a balanced diet, it should get all the vitamins it needs from its food, and some animals even make many vitamins within their own bodies. But sometimes, even with a good diet, an animal won't get everything it needs, and zoos will need to give it supplements (extra nutrients).

In zoos, vitamins usually aren't given to animals in the form of pills. Although your parents might hand you a vitamin pill and tell you to chew it up, a zoo animal probably wouldn't be so cooperative. Instead, zookeepers often have to find special ways to hide vitamins—whether in tablet, powder, liquid, or paste form—inside an animal's food to make sure it gets eaten. Sometimes they use foods an animal really likes just for this purpose; for example, hiding vitamins for an elephant in a tasty fruit or loaf of bread.

Medicines for elephants, gorillas, and other animals are also often hidden in sweet foods such as apples. The core of an apple is removed, and liquid

When Asian elephants need to take medicine, keepers often disguise its bitter taste by hiding it inside a sweet food, such as an apple.

or powdered medicine is put in the hole; the core is then replaced. The keeper or veterinarian will hand-feed the apples to the animal. Like medicine for people, animal medicines can sometimes taste pretty bad, so it helps if it's hidden inside something sweet.

How Reptiles Get Their Vitamins

It's believed that in the wild, when lizards and other insect-eating animals (insectivores) grub in the dirt for food, they may also get some much needed minerals from the soil. In captivity, insectivores are fed very clean insects to ensure that they stay healthy. But this means that they may not get all the minerals they need, especially calcium. To make sure that these animals are getting a balanced diet in zoos, the insects they eat are often nutrient loaded. Calcium-rich food is given to the insects for a few days before they're fed to other animals, and extra calcium-rich limestone and powdered vitamins are sprinkled on the insects as well.

Insects and minerals aren't the only things lizards need to stay healthy in captivity. It was recently discovered that many reptiles need to be kept under a special kind of light. Many tortoises and lizards, especially animals from warm desert areas, normally spend a lot of time basking in the sun. To get the beneficial effects of the sun in captivity, they need to be under special indoor full-spectrum lights, which re-create the different rays of the sun. These lights help the reptiles to properly form vitamin D inside their skin and

Many reptiles in zoos, such as these tortoises, are kept under special full-spectrum lights that offer the same beneficial effects as natural sunlight.

absorb calcium into their bodies so they will grow correctly and form strong shells and bones. Full-spectrum light is especially important for young, growing animals, but adults are provided with it, too. The full-spectrum lights aren't noticeable because they blend in with the regular fluorescent lights that are used in exhibits.

What Makes a Pink Flamingo Pink?

A lot of animals in zoos have very unusual feeding requirements. In order to keep its feathers pink, for example, a flamingo needs to eat special foods. In the wild, flamingos eat plants and animals, such as shrimp and other small crustaceans, that contain coloring agents called carotenoids, which keep the birds' feathers pink. (Crustaceans are water-dwelling animals with hard outer shells.) But in captivity flamingos are fed a different diet, so zoos have to add coloring agents. Some are

Young flamingos are dependent on their parents for nourishment until they can filter feed. This involves holding their bills upside down in the water, swaying them back and forth, and filtering out bits of food.

artificial and are added to the food in powdered form, and some, such as carrot juice, are natural. If the flamingos aren't given coloring agents, their feathers turn white. Although this isn't harmful, these birds don't breed (produce young) well if their feathers aren't pink. Many other birds with red feathers, such as the beautiful scarlet ibis, are also fed carotenoids to keep their feathers bright.

CHAPTER FOUR

HOW DO YOU NURSE A BABY PORCUPINE?

Mothers know best how to feed and care for their young, and in zoos most animals raise their own babies. There are times, however, when zoo caretakers have to step in and hand rear baby animals, such as when the mother is ill or has died. And in some cases, hand rearing is routine. Many bird-exhibit areas either don't have enough room for extra animals or are designed for adults only, so baby birds hatched in the zoo are often raised in bird nurseries. Most reptile babies don't need care from their parents—either in the wild or in captivity—so in zoos the young are moved to separate quarters right from the start.

But how do zoos know how to feed and care for these animals on a daily basis? And what are the differences between caring for mammal, bird, and reptile young?

In the Incubator

When a baby mammal is taken from its mother to be hand reared at the Bronx Zoo, it's generally brought to the zoo's animal hospital, or health center. There it's raised by experienced veterinary technicians. The baby is cared for until it's strong enough to return to its exhibit.

Most of these infants are placed in incubators, where temperature, humidity (moisture in the air), and oxygen levels can be carefully controlled, and

This tiny marmoset spends its first days in an incubator. It's taken out regularly to be fed and cared for.

the tiny babies can be kept warm and secure. If you've ever been to a hospital nursery, you may have seen some human babies in incubators, and these are the same little glass-enclosed beds that the zoo uses. The incubators' sides have small openings so the technicians can slide their hands inside to reach the animals, and the top can be opened as well.

Animals that are too large for incubators are usually put into wooden boxes with open tops; heat lamps are placed nearby for warmth. Technicians take the baby animals out of the incubators regularly to feed and care for them. Often they put some sort of soft doll in with the babies to give them something to cuddle in place of their mother and siblings (brothers and sisters).

Getting Used to a Bottle

Since drinking from a bottle isn't natural for animals, they may not be comfortable with it right away. Usually a newborn will accept a bottle more easily than an infant that's been with its mother for several days and has already nursed from a natural nipple. When technicians begin to bottle-feed a

A baby hippopotamus is bottle-fed a milk formula created especially to meet its specific nutritional requirements.

baby, they have to be careful not to force the bottle into the infant's mouth, because if the animal gets scared, it won't eat. It can take two or three days with some animals, such as fawns (baby deer), to get them to drink from a bottle. First the caretakers have to gain the fawn's trust. They might gently scratch its fur, imitating what a mother deer would do in grooming her young. Then they might try dipping their fingers into some milk formula and letting the baby lick it off. Once the baby gets used to the taste of the formula, it will be more willing to try the bottle.

Different mammal species need different types of milk, so formulas have to be created specially for each animal. A wolf pup, for instance, needs extra-rich milk, while a foal, or baby horse, needs a thinner milk that's high in sugar and water but low in fat and protein.

How Often Are Babies Fed?

The number of daily feedings given depends on the type of animal. Baby rabbits need to eat only two or three times a day, but baby deer may need to eat eight times a day. The feeding schedule is

Formulas vary from rich and high fat to thin and more sugary, depending on individual animals' needs. For baby animals, such as this red panda, it can take a little time to get used to drinking from a bottle.

generally related to how rich the milk formula is. Thinner, more watery milks digest easily and quickly and have to be offered more often. The amount given at each feeding also varies and is based on the baby's body weight.

At some zoos, such as the Bronx Zoo, veterinarians who live on the grounds take turns with night rounds at the hospital. They check in during the night on all the hospitalized animals and feed any that need it. Middle-of-the-night feedings are given only to newborns and are stopped after the first few weeks. From then on, infants are fed throughout the day, starting at 6 A.M. and ending at 11 P.M. Young animals are weighed daily (before feeding) to make sure they are growing.

Handling Prickly Animals

You might wonder how veterinarians and technicians feed hard-to-handle animals, such as baby porcupines with those prickly quills. The answer is, very carefully. Although most porcupines aren't aggressive animals, they are born with small, sharp quills that can hurt. If technicians

For the first week of a baby porcupine's life, it eats only formula. After that, carrots, greens, yams, bananas, and rodent chow are slowly added to its diet.

have to handle a porcupine, they place one hand on the animal's underside, where the quills are just stiff hair but not so prickly, and the other hand on the animal's tail. Often they wear protective gloves. Porcupines, by the way, can't shoot their quills, as was once believed. Instead, when they are in danger, they rub up against an animal and their quills become imbedded in the animal's skin.

Hand Starting Gorilla Babies

Lowland gorillas are an endangered species, and about one out of four babies born at zoos in the United States is cared for by humans, which for these animals is called hand starting. They are raised by very nurturing people, called surrogate (or substitute) mothers. Hand starting helps to ensure that abandoned babies will survive. Gorillas are social animals and are generally very caring toward others of their own species. Some gorillas, however, make poor mothers. In these cases, or when illness on the mother's or baby's part keeps the bond from forming properly between parent and child, the baby will be hand started. Because

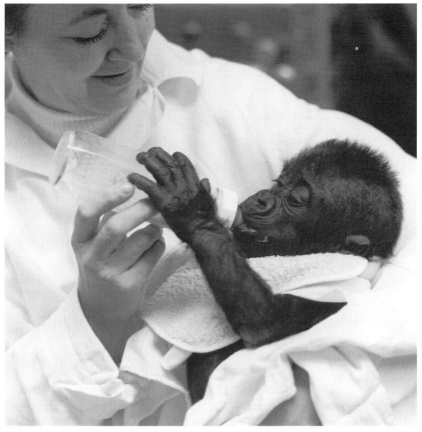

Baby lowland gorillas need the same kind of care as human babies do. In zoos, surrogate mothers sometimes provide that care until the youngsters join adult gorilla groups between the ages of one and two.

gorillas are closely related to humans, the things humans do naturally with babies, such as holding, nursing, and carrying them around, is what gorilla mothers do, too.

To make sure that the infants will be able to relate to other gorillas when they get older, a surrogate mother generally hand starts at least two baby gorillas together. This is called peer rearing. Youngsters are introduced to older gorillas at the age of one to two. Most adult gorillas, both males and females, will instinctively care for older babies—even those adults that may not be good with newborns.

The Bird Nursery

Birds are often hand reared in zoos. If the parents are unable to rear the chicks safely, the exhibit is too small, or there's too much competition for food, the chicks will be hand reared. The Bronx Zoo follows a general routine for hand rearing baby birds. Eggs are brought to the hatcher room and put into a special incubator—the kind that's used for hatching chicken eggs. This type of incubator has sliding drawers where many eggs can be placed together. The temperature is kept at around 95 degrees Fahrenheit, and the eggs are rotated regularly.

When the egg is just about to hatch, it's put into the hatcher, which is a big box with water at the bottom. Here the temperature is kept quite high, and the air is extremely moist. The keepers know an egg is ready to hatch when they hear a pipping sound from inside the shell. The bird is using its egg tooth (a sharp point on its beak) to start breaking out of the shell. The egg must be kept moist; otherwise, it's difficult for the chick to break out. After it hatches, the chick is moved to the brooder room. There it will be placed either in a typical human-baby incubator or into a brooder box—a wooden box with a heat lamp in the corner that chicks can go under.

Birds such as pheasants or cranes are precocial, which means they can care for themselves after hatching. These species are put into a brooder

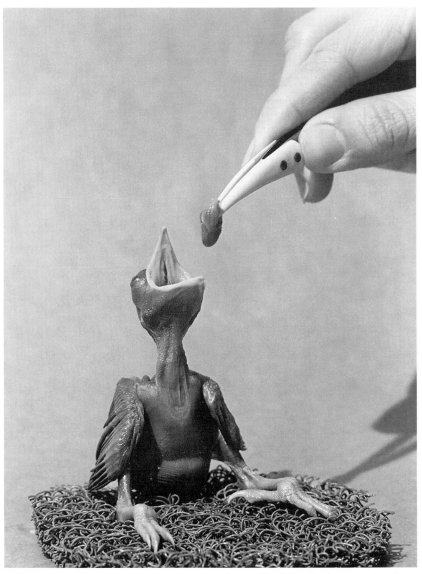

Here a keeper uses a tool that resembles a beak to feed a tiny bird of paradise.

box. Temperature in a brooder box varies depending on the species that's occupying it. Altricial (undeveloped) birds, such as birds of paradise or kingfishers, need a lot of care after hatching. They are placed in incubators and at first are hand-fed every two to three hours. If one or two birds of the same species or of closely related species hatch at the same time, they can go into the incubator together.

Inside the incubator, keepers put a little nest box that's lined and covered with soft tissue paper. Other paper is placed underneath the box. All of these papers are replaced as they get soiled.

Raising Pink Pigeons

Some birds, such as pink pigeons, need special care. Although they do lay eggs, pink pigeons don't seem to make good parents and sometimes build their nests in unsafe places. The male and

In zoos, pink-pigeon chicks are sometimes raised by their close relatives, ring-necked doves. At first, the doves feed the babies a food called crop milk; later, keepers add seeds, fruits, and greens.

female birds often fight over who is going to sit on the eggs, and end up breaking them.

Pink pigeons are one of the rarest pigeons in the world. At the Bronx Zoo, pink-pigeon eggs are routinely taken from the mothers to help ensure that all the chicks survive. Instead of being hand reared by humans, however, ring-necked doves, which are close relatives of the pink pigeon, act as surrogate parents. After the pink pigeon lays its egg, the egg is placed under a ring-necked dove to hatch. Even though these doves are much smaller than pink pigeons, they are capable of keeping the chick fed. When an animal of one species rears one of another species, it's called cross fostering.

When Reptiles Hatch

Most reptile babies in zoos are cared for in special nurseries. There are several reasons why this is done. First, reptile exhibits are usually designed only for adults. Second, reptiles are capable of caring for themselves after hatching and don't need to stay with their parents. And third, the habitats young reptiles need to live in, as well as their food requirements, are often very different from those of adults.

There is another important reason why reptile eggs, including those of turtles, crocodiles, and some lizards, are regularly taken out of the adult exhibits. Keepers need to control the temperature at which the eggs develop. Amazingly, with some reptiles the temperature of the air and soil that the eggs incubate in determines if the baby will be male or female. Being able to control the number of each sex hatched can be important, especially when a zoo is breeding endangered animals. It wouldn't be very good if only females hatched or only males—you need a balance of the two.

How Does Good Nutrition Help Save Endangered Animals?

Zoos provide homes for thousands of different animal species, many of which are endangered. They work hard to make sure the animals they care for stay healthy and have healthy babies. Many rare animals that didn't do well living in zoos years ago are thriving now, and proper care, good diets, and naturalistic exhibits that have the look and feel of animals' homes in the wild are three of the key reasons.

Many species of animals are extinct in nature and survive only in zoos, and more will become so in the future because of loss of natural habitats. Good nutrition will continue to play an important role in helping zoos preserve animal species.

Selected Animal Diets

Animal	Diet in the Wild	Zoo Diet
MAMMALS		
African dormouse	Seeds, nuts, fruits, insects	Kale, rodent chow, mixed seeds
African lion	Antelopes, young giraffes, carrion, zebras, birds, wild hogs	Commercial feline food, chicken; knucklebones (for chewing)
Asian elephant	Grass, wood, bark, leaves, shoots, fruits	Grass hays, grains, browse, leaves; carrots, apples, bread as treats
Black rhinoceros	Twigs, bushes, tree branches	Horse-hay pellets, mixed legumes and grass hays, browse

Animal   Diet in the Wild   Zoo Diet

Animal	Diet in the Wild	Zoo Diet
California sea lion	Squid, fish	Supplemented mackerel, herring, capelin fish
European ferret	Rodents, birds	Feline diet, some vegetables (carrots, greens); mice as treats
Giant panda	Mostly bamboo; some other plants	Mainly bamboo; also steamed bread or gruel made of rice and other grains
Grizzly bear	Vegetation, small rodents, fish	Omnivore biscuits, chicken parts, fish; honey as treat

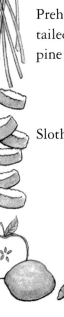

Lowland gorilla | Leaves, shoots, stems, branches, herbs, berries, wild celery | Yams, carrots, celery, greens, primate biscuits and canned food, bananas, oranges, apples, browse; grains, popcorn, sunflower seeds, peanut butter, and peanuts as treats

Prehensile-tailed porcupine | Leaves, fruits, bark, nuts, insects, reptiles | High-fiber biscuits, greens, yams, carrots, apples; wood or bone (for gnawing)

Sloth bear | Fruits, berries, roots, honey, carcasses, small animals, including ants, termites, and wild bees | Four days a week: omnivore biscuits, apples, oranges, grapes; three days a week: mix of dog meal, peanut

Animal Diet in the Wild Zoo Diet

Animal	Diet in the Wild	Zoo Diet
		butter, honey, apple juice, and water; crickets and mealworms as treats
Tufted deer	Grass, leaves, buds	Pellets, mixed grass/legume hay
White-cheeked gibbon	Fruits, leaves, flowers, insects	Canned primate food, high-fiber biscuits, oranges, bananas, apples, greens; crickets, small mice, peanuts as treats

BIRDS

Amazon parrot	Fruits, seeds, nuts, green leaves, pollen	Bird pellets, seeds, vegetables, fruits

| Chilean flamingo | Aquatic plants and animals | Mixture of bird pellets, water, and coloring agent (to keep feathers pink) |

Fishing eagle — Fish, aquatic birds, carrion — Fish; bird-of-prey diet

Lesser and red birds of paradise — Fruits, berries, insects, frogs, lizards — Low-iron grain pellets, fruits, vegetables, greens, insects, mealworms

Ring-necked dove/pink pigeon — Seeds, grains — Bird pellets, seeds, mixed salad of fruits and greens

Scarlet ibis — Small crabs, mollusks, aquatic insects; some fish, snails, algae — Dog kibble, supplemented meat diet, water, coloring agent

Animal	Diet in the Wild	Zoo Diet
REPTILES		
Bornean pond turtle	Fruits, aquatic plants, fish, crustaceans, mollusks, carrion found in the water	Vegetables, fish, earthworms, mice, crustaceans, turtle chow
Cuban crocodile	Mostly fish; some birds and small mammals	Rats, mice, chicken parts
Eastern hognose snake	Mainly toads; some frogs and other amphibians	Toad-scented mice
Gopher snake	Rodents, birds, young lizards	Small rats, mice
South American boa constrictor	Small birds, mammals, and lizards	Rats, mice

Spitting cobra	Rodents, birds, other reptiles	Rats, mice
Water monitor lizard	Mammals, birds, lizards, amphibians, fish, snakes, insects, crustaceans	Rats, mice, chicks, trout

In addition to the foods listed here, many zoo animals' diets contain added vitamin and mineral supplements.

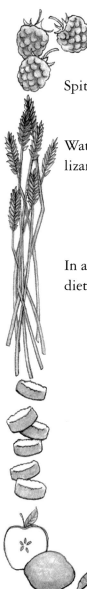

INDEX

(Page numbers in *italic* refer to illustrations.)

DATE			